Marilyn

MONROE

NORMA JEANE'S DREAM

Marilyn MONROE

NORMA JEANE'S DREAM

Katherine E. Krohn

LERNER PUBLICATIONS COMPANY ▪ MINNEAPOLIS

CONNOLLY.

This book is dedicated to my big brother, Bill Krohn, who made me dedicate this book to him. I would also like to thank my friend and editor, LeeAnne Engfer, for her skill, humor, and unfailing insight.

Editor's Note: The name given to Marilyn Monroe at birth appears in various sources with the following spellings: "Norma Jean" and "Norma Jeane," "Mortensen" and "Mortenson." Using what we consider the most authoritative sources, including Norma Jeane's own signature, we have elected to use the spelling Norma Jeane Mortensen.

Library of Congress Cataloging-in-Publication Data

Krohn, Katherine E.
    Marilyn Monroe: Norma Jeane's dream / Katherine E. Krohn.
       p. cm.
    Includes bibliographical references and index.
    Summary: A biography of the screen icon, from her early days as an orphan to her rise to stardom; includes discussion of her film career, marriages, and tragic death.
    ISBN 0-8225-4930-1 (alk. paper)
       1. Monroe, Marilyn, 1926–1962—Juvenile literature. 2. Motion picture actors and actresses—United States—Biography—Juvenile literature. [1. Monroe, Marilyn, 1926–1962. 2. Actors and actresses. 3. Women—Biography.] I. Title.
PN2287.M69K76 1997
791.43'028'092—dc20
[B]   96–26526

Manufactured in the United States of America
1 2 3 4 5 6 – JR – 02 01 00 99 98 97

CONTENTS

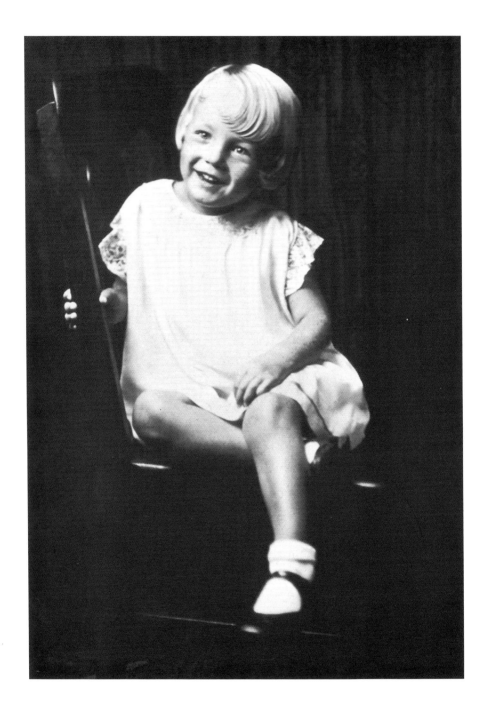

CHAPTER ONE

NORMA JEANE

"NORMA JEANE, LOOK UP IN THE SKY!"

The young girl tilted her head toward the clouds. A small, two-seater airplane flew close to her house, so close that the windows rattled and her dog, Tippy, barked.

The sound of the engine drowned out Norma Jeane's shrieks of delight as the airplane circled her house once again. This time, the pilot leaned out of the plane and waved to the six-year-old girl. Norma Jeane saw that he wore goggles and a thick leather jacket, typical gear for a pilot in the early 1930s. A long white scarf, knotted tightly around his neck, blew behind him in the wind.

Norma Jeane didn't know that her mother, Gladys, had arranged the special event. Gladys worked as a film cutter for Columbia Studios, a movie studio in Hollywood, California. She had asked a friend, a delivery pilot for the studio, to wave hello to Norma Jeane the next time he flew over her house.

Gladys didn't have the opportunity to see her daughter very often. She didn't have enough money to take care of

Norma Jeane, and she had been forced to place her in a foster home. She wanted to do something very special for her daughter's birthday. Gladys knew that Norma Jeane would love the surprise.

Norma Jeane would have been even more surprised to know that she herself would be working in Hollywood one day, and her job would be like no other. Norma Jeane Mortensen would one day change her name to "Marilyn Monroe," and she would be a radiantly beautiful, world-famous movie star.

Norma Jeane Mortensen was born on the first day of June, 1926, in the charity ward of Los Angeles General Hospital. Norma Jeane was a healthy baby with big blue eyes and strawberry blond hair.

Norma Jeane's mother, Gladys Pearl Baker Mortensen, was a delicate woman with red hair. While Gladys was ambitious, she was also down on her luck. At twenty-six, Gladys had been married and divorced twice.

In 1915, when Gladys was only fourteen, she married a man named Jasper Baker. (With her mother's encouragement, Gladys lied about her age and said she was eighteen.) Gladys and Jasper had two children, Berniece and Jackie. One day Gladys came home from work and her husband and children were gone. Jasper left only a short note behind: he had taken the children to another state, and Gladys would never see them again.

In Los Angeles, Gladys tried to pull her life together. She worked long hours at her job at the film studio. She

Norma Jeane as a baby

told acquaintances that her children had died, so she wouldn't have to talk about her painful loss.

In the late 1800s, a handful of inventors across the world experimented with "moving pictures." They made special cameras and projectors that put still photographs in motion. In 1895, the Lumière brothers showed their first film in France. That year, films were also screened for the first time in London, Berlin, and New York. The public raved about the new and entertaining sensation.

Top: *Hollywood in about 1930.* Bottom: *The "talkies" were still new in 1929, when a cameraman and sound engineer recorded the MGM lion roaring.*

In 1913, motion picture studios opened for business in a small suburb of Los Angeles called Hollywood. The new film industry created many jobs for technical crews, builders, directors, writers, and actors. Each year brought technological advances to motion pictures. In 1927, the first sound movie was made, *The Jazz Singer,* starring Al Jolson. (Until then, movies were silent.)

Gladys Baker considered herself fortunate to have a job in Hollywood. She liked splicing, or cutting, the film, an essential step of movie production. She cut frames, or pieces, of film that editors used to put together the final movie. As images of popular actors of the 1920s passed through her fingers—stars like Rudolph Valentino, Greta Garbo, Gloria Swanson, and Charlie Chaplin—Gladys felt proud to be part of such an exciting industry.

The 1920s in the United States—the "Roaring Twenties"—was known as a fun, free time, especially for women. American women had recently won the right to vote. "Flappers" in knee-length dresses kicked up their heels and danced the Charleston, a fast ballroom dance. Many women modeled themselves after the film stars they admired. They painted their faces with rouge and lipstick and changed the color of their hair. Gladys dyed her hair a dazzling shade of red, to resemble the sassy screen star Clara Bow.

In 1924 Gladys remarried. Martin Edward Mortensen was a tall, handsome man. Unfortunately, the marriage didn't last long. Gladys and Martin divorced just a few months after the wedding.

Several months after the couple parted ways, Gladys discovered she was pregnant. She said that Mortensen was the father of her baby, but at the time she became pregnant she had been dating a few men. No one would ever know for sure who Norma Jeane's real father was.

Soon to be a single parent, Gladys didn't know how she would care for her baby and keep her job at the studio. Gladys's own mother, Della Monroe, was ill and couldn't help with the new baby. Gladys had no other family and few options—in the 1920s, day care centers and preschools did not exist.

Twelve days after Norma Jeane came into the world, Gladys placed her in a foster home. She paid Ida and Albert Bolender five dollars a week to care for her baby. The couple lived across the street from Gladys's mother. Gladys visited Norma Jeane when she could. She promised to take her back to live with her someday.

The Bolenders lived in a small frame house in the working-class town of Hawthorne, California, a few miles south of Los Angeles. They believed that "children should be seen and not heard." As Norma Jeane grew, her lively personality began to emerge. She loved to sing and dance. Because of the Bolenders' strict religious beliefs, they did not approve of Norma Jeane's behavior. They thought that dancing was sinful. "You're wicked, Norma Jeane," Ida scolded. "You better be careful, or you know where you'll go."

Every month an inspector from Children's Social Services stopped by the Bolenders to check on Norma Jeane.

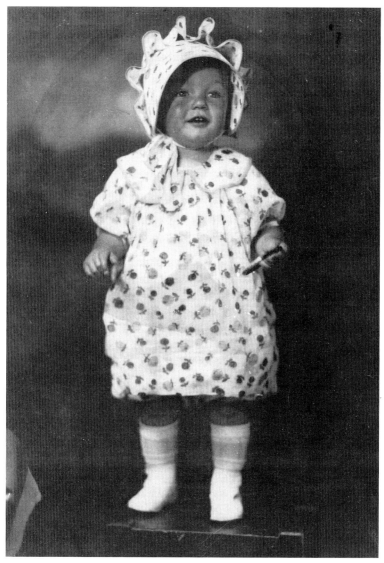

As a baby, Norma Jeane lived with a foster family.

"She never asked me any questions but would pick up my foot and look at the bottom of my shoes. If my shoe bottoms weren't worn through I was reported in thriving condition," Norma Jeane said later.

Norma Jeane felt confused. Because she had lived with the Bolenders since she was a baby and rarely saw her mother, she came to think of the Bolenders as her real parents. Once Norma Jeane called Ida "Mama."

> NORMA JEANE DIDN'T FEEL AS IF SHE REALLY KNEW HER MOTHER. GLADYS RARELY SMILED, AND SHE NEVER KISSED OR HUGGED NORMA JEANE.

"Don't call me mama. You're old enough to know better," Ida said. "I'm not related to you in any way. You just board here."

Meanwhile, Norma Jeane wondered about her birth mother. Would Gladys come and take her to live with her, as she had promised?

Sometimes Gladys took Norma Jeane to her Los Angeles apartment for a weekend visit. Norma Jeane liked these excursions to her mother's home—she enjoyed any kind of adventure—but she didn't feel as if she really knew her mother. Gladys rarely smiled, and she never kissed or hugged Norma Jeane.

"We never had any kind of relationship," Norma Jeane recalled. "I didn't see her very often. To me she was just the woman with the red hair."

On one visit, Norma Jeane was lying in bed and turning the pages of a book. "Stop making so much noise, Norma," Gladys said. The sound of the pages turning made her nervous.

Norma Jeane admired the framed photograph of a man that hung on her mother's wall. "Whenever I visited my mother I would stand looking at this photograph and hold my breath for fear she would order me to stop looking," she remembered. "I had found out that people always ordered me to stop doing anything I liked to do."

Norma Jeane thought the man was very handsome. He had dark skin and hair, a thin mustache, and a hat worn tipped to the side. Norma Jeane thought he looked like Clark Gable, her favorite Hollywood actor.

One day Gladys lifted Norma Jeane so that she could see the photograph better. She told her that the man was Norma Jeane's father. Most likely, the man wasn't related to Norma Jeane. But the portrait comforted Norma Jeane, because it gave her something she had never had before—hope. Despite what some people said, that she was an "illegitimate child," she did have a father. And, she thought, he might come for her some day and take her to a happier home.

Norma Jeane at four years old (with an unidentified playmate)

CHAPTER TWO

THE ORPHAN

NORMA JEANE LONGED FOR A REAL HOME, WITH parents who loved her and each other. She felt like a maid in her foster home. Instead of child's play, her days were filled with chores: washing dishes and mopping floors, doing loads of laundry and running errands.

While Norma Jeane wished for a loving home, her mother was suffering from mental illness. Some people believe that Gladys's job, which involved the daily handling of the toxic chemicals used in film developing, may have caused brain damage.

In the 1930s, strict health laws for the workplace did not exist. Gladys labored eight to twelve hours a day in a small, windowless room. She breathed vapors that seeped from open chemical bottles and tubes of film cement.

At the time, the United States was in the middle of the Great Depression, an economic crisis that affected many lives. Many people had trouble finding work. Gladys was happy to have a job—any job, particularly a "glamorous"

An early film editing machine

job at a movie studio. Though she had developed excruci-
ating headaches and unexplained chest pains, she didn't
dare complain to her employer. She knew that plenty of
people would have taken her place gladly.

Despite her health problems, Gladys held on to her
dream of making a home for herself and her daughter. In
the fall of 1933, Gladys came to take Norma Jeane from
the Bolenders.

Norma Jeane had lived with the Bolenders for seven
years. Though they were strict foster parents, she had
grown attached to the couple and their adopted son,

Lester. Unsure and a little frightened, Norma Jeane silently packed the dresses that Ida had sewn for her and said good-bye to the Bolenders.

Gladys took out a bank loan to buy a charming white bungalow with a white picket fence located at 6812 Arbol Drive in Hollywood. Norma Jeane was excited to see that the furnished, three-bedroom house even came with a baby grand piano. She took lessons with Miss Marion Miller, a music teacher in the neighborhood.

To help make ends meet, Gladys rented out part of the house to some friends in the movie business. The boarders, a lively English family of three, played bit parts in Hollywood films. The family taught Norma Jeane how to hula dance and play cards. Once they gave Norma Jeane whiskey bottles to play with. "Life became pretty casual and tumultuous, quite a change from [the Bolenders]," she remembered. "Because of that religious upbringing I'd had, I was kind of shocked . . . I spent hours praying for them."

A few months after Gladys purchased the house, her grandfather died, and she fell into a major depression. Gladys's dreams for herself and her daughter also collapsed. In early 1934, Gladys had a serious breakdown. Too unstable to hold a job or to care for Norma Jeane, Gladys was taken to a rest home in Santa Monica.

"For a long time . . . I could no longer daydream about anything," Norma Jeane recalled. "I kept hearing my mother screaming and laughing as they led her out of the home she had tried to build for me."

Over the next several months, Gladys's condition grew worse. Eventually she was transferred to the psychiatric ward of Los Angeles General Hospital. She would remain in psychiatric hospitals most of the time for the rest of her life.

Seven-year-old Norma Jeane was on her own again. For a while, Gladys's best friend, Grace McKee, a film librarian at Columbia Studios, took care of Norma Jeane. Grace loved Norma Jeane and wanted to adopt her. For a few months, while Grace waited for the courts to approve the adoption, Norma Jeane was placed in foster care.

In the meantime, Grace met a new man. Ervin "Doc" Goddard, an engineer and amateur inventor, wanted to marry Grace. Unfortunately, he did not want to adopt Norma Jeane—at least not right away. Because he already had three children from a previous marriage, he didn't think he could afford to raise another child.

> I SAW A BIG BLACK SIGN WITH BRIGHT GOLD LETTERING....LOS ANGELES ORPHANS HOME. I TRIED TO TELL THEM I WASN'T AN ORPHAN.

On September 13, 1935, Grace drove Norma Jeane to her new home. As Grace pulled up the driveway of the institution, a red brick Colonial mansion, Norma Jeane began to cry. "I remember when I got out of the car, and my feet absolutely couldn't move on the sidewalk," Norma Jeane said. "I saw a big black sign with bright gold lettering." The sign said Los Angeles Orphans Home. "I tried to tell them I wasn't an orphan,"she said.

As Grace held back her own tears, she dragged Norma Jeane through the orphanage doors. Grace assured Norma Jeane that as soon as she "got a few things straightened out" she would return for her. Nine-year-old Norma Jeane felt frightened and abandoned.

Norma Jeane later claimed that she was treated badly at the orphanage. Some people believe, however, that she exaggerated about how difficult the conditions were at the children's home.

All the orphans had to wear uniforms—a white shirt, blue skirt, and ugly black shoes with heavy soles. Because Norma Jeane was one of the older children in the home, she was assigned more chores than most of the others. She washed dishes—dozens of cups, plates, forks, knives, and spoons. "I did it three times a day, seven days a week," she said. "But it wasn't so bad. It was worse to scrub out the toilets."

The children were paid five cents a week for their labor, and they were encouraged to put a penny in the church collection plate each Sunday. With her remaining money, Norma Jeane usually bought herself a hair ribbon, something pretty to brighten up her dull uniform.

Once or twice a week, Grace McKee visited Norma Jeane at the orphanage. Though Grace didn't have much money, sometimes she would splurge and treat Norma Jeane to lunch and a movie. Other times she took her to have her hair styled. "Aunt Grace" was a kind woman. "She was the first person who ever patted my head or touched my cheek," Norma Jeane said.

Occasionally, in the months before Grace married Doc, Norma Jeane would stay with her in her small house in Los Angeles. When Grace was laid off from her job at Columbia Studios, she cut corners and tried to make do. Sometimes she lived on bread and milk alone. For twenty-five cents, Norma Jeane and Grace could buy a bag of stale bread from the neighborhood bakery.

At nine, Norma Jeane was big for her age. Because she was often unhappy, she rarely smiled. Some children didn't like her and made fun of her plain, well-worn clothing. They pointed at her and giggled and called her "dumb."

Grace noticed Norma Jeane's awkwardness and tried to make her feel better about herself. She smiled at Norma Jeane and smoothed her slightly frizzy, shoulder-length hair. She assured Norma Jeane that she would be a beautiful woman one day—maybe even a movie star. "Her words made me so happy that the stale bread tasted like cream puffs," Norma Jeane recalled.

Back at the orphanage, Norma Jeane sometimes climbed the stairs to the roof. She liked to look at the big water tower at the film studio where her mother had once worked. "Sometimes that made me cry, because I felt so lonely," Norma Jeane remembered. "But it also became . . . my fantasy—to work where movies were made. When I told this to Grace, she almost danced for joy."

The orphanage sponsored occasional outings for the children. "The only time I was happy was when they took us to a movie," Norma Jeane said. "I loved movies . . . . The stars were my friends."

*Movie theaters in the 1930s and 1940s were designed as
lavish "palaces," with gala festivities to celebrate the opening
of new pictures.*

Like many moviegoers of the 1930s, Norma Jeane admired the sultry, platinum-blond movie star Jean Harlow. Harlow was very beautiful, but she wasn't self-conscious about her looks. She was confident and independent. Norma Jeane wanted to be just like her.

Norma Jeane often took refuge in daydreams to comfort herself. In a make-believe world, she could imagine a life

Jean Harlow was a popular film actress when Norma Jeane was young. Norma Jeane's "Aunt Grace" hoped that Norma Jeane would grow up to be a movie star like Jean Harlow.

for herself that was glamorous and happy. Most of all, she imagined that she was incredibly beautiful.

"Daydreaming made my work easier," she said. "When I was waiting on the table . . . where I lived, I would day-dream I was a waitress in an elegant hotel, dressed in a white waitress uniform, and everybody who entered the grand dining room where I was serving would stop to look at me and openly admire me."

Norma Jeane craved attention of any kind—it probably made her feel loved. "I never dreamed of anyone loving me as I saw other children loved," she said. "That was too big a stretch for my imagination. I compromised by dreaming of my attracting someone's attention . . . of having people look at me and say my name."

Throughout her life, Norma Jeane would again and again use her beauty and her body to win love and attention from others. She didn't realize that a woman's power lies in the choices she makes for herself and her ability to act on her decisions.

Norma Jeane Baker in tenth grade

CHAPTER THREE

TEEN YEARS

OVER THE YEARS, NORMA JEANE FLOATED FROM home to home like a boat adrift. But, always, she had one constant visitor. "Aunt Grace" visited Norma Jeane at least once a week. She cheered her "niece" with small gifts like flowers and chocolates, along with the promise that Norma Jeane could live with her one day.

In the summer of 1938, shortly after Norma Jeane's twelfth birthday, Aunt Grace brought some surprising news. Grace's aunt, Ana Lower, wanted Norma Jeane to live with her in her home in West Los Angeles. Norma Jeane was apprehensive. She didn't know Mrs. Lower. And she would have to adjust to a new home in a new neighborhood. Worst of all, she would have to start over again at a new school.

Gravel beat against the side of the car and dust flew in all directions as Aunt Grace drove through the Sawtelle district toward Ana Lower's house. Norma Jeane's heart raced and her stomach ached. Would Ana Lower like her? Or would she reject her and send her back to the

orphanage? Norma Jeane noticed the neighborhood's run-
down, ranch-style homes. Everything looked strange and
unfamiliar. She tried not to cry as she stared at the un-
paved road ahead.

Fortunately, Norma Jeane's fears did not last long. As
Grace pulled into the bumpy driveway, a smiling, heavy-
set woman in her late fifties hurried out of the house.
Ana Lower welcomed Norma Jeane with a big hug and
helped her with her suitcase.

Norma Jeane quickly grew attached to Ana Lower.
"Aunt Ana" was a wise woman with a strong religious
faith. She believed in the power of positive thinking.
"She was a wonderful human being," Norma Jeane remembered. "I once wrote a poem about her . . . It was
called 'I love her.' She never hurt me, not once. She
couldn't. She was all kindness and all love."

Norma Jeane tried to make friends at her new school,
Emerson Junior High. But she felt like she didn't fit in
with the other students. She was tall for her age, shy and
awkward. One day at school some girls made fun of the
dress Norma Jeane was wearing. Crushed, she ran home
in tears.

"It doesn't make any difference if other children make
fun of you, or of your clothes, or where you live," Aunt
Ana told Norma Jeane as she hugged her. "Always remember, dear: it's what you are that really counts. Just
keep being yourself, honey, that's all that matters."

With Ana's guidance, Norma Jeane began to think of
her future in a different way—she didn't have to be a sad

orphan for the rest of her life. Indeed, if she set her mind to it, she could be a writer, or a great athlete, or, she joked to herself, even a famous movie star. Loved and encouraged by Aunt Ana, Norma Jeane grew more hopeful and self-assured.

Two years later, fourteen-year-old Norma Jeane welcomed more good news. Aunt Grace had moved into a big new house in the San Fernando Valley near Los Angeles. At last, Grace had financial stability, and she wanted Norma Jeane to live with her.

Promising to visit Aunt Ana on the weekends, Norma Jeane moved again. She had always dreamed of living with Aunt Grace, and since she had lived with Grace's Aunt Ana, Norma Jeane felt closer than ever to the family.

Norma Jeane quickly blended into her new household, which included Grace's husband, Ervin S. "Doc" Goddard, and his three children from a former marriage, Eleanor (nicknamed Bebe), Fritz, and Josephine. The family also included a cocker spaniel and two Persian cats.

Norma Jeane liked Bebe most of all. The two girls, who were close in age, hit it off right away and soon shared secrets and clothing. Bebe was popular at school. She proudly introduced "Normi," as she affectionately called Norma Jeane, to her friends. Before long, Norma Jeane had friends, too, for the first time in her life.

With the Goddards, Norma Jeane felt a happy sense of belonging, but she often thought of her mother. Gladys was still in a psychiatric institution. Her mental health had not improved. Norma Jeane didn't know if she would ever see her mother again, but she had no choice other than to carry on with her life.

Van Nuys High School was much bigger than any school Norma Jeane had ever attended. She had a variety of classes, such as home economics and general mathematics, but her favorite subject was English. She kept a journal and liked to write poetry.

While Norma Jeane had talent as a writer, she also had athletic ability. Throughout her high school years, she excelled in track and volleyball.

At Emerson Junior High, Norma Jeane had acted a small part in a school play. But at Van Nuys High, she showed no interest in acting. Instead, she preferred to participate in sports. Her interest in drama showed only in her frequent excursions to the local movie theater.

In 1939, the classic film *Gone With the Wind* was released. Norma Jeane walked the three miles to school to save ten cents in bus fare—the price of admission to the theater. Her heart pounded as Clark Gable appeared on the screen as the dashing Rhett Butler. Even as a teenager, Norma Jeane still fantasized that Gable was her long-lost father.

One of Norma Jeane's classmates at Van Nuys, a girl named Jane Russell, won admiration for her starring role in the school play. Several years later, Russell found fame as a leading lady in Hollywood.

Norma Jeane also attracted attention at school—but not because of anything she was doing. Almost overnight, the skinny, awkward girl developed into a strong and graceful, strikingly beautiful young woman. Boys stared at her,

Norma Jeane's idol, Clark Gable, starred with Vivian Leigh in Gone With the Wind, *released in 1939, when Norma Jeane was in high school.*

followed close behind her, and asked to carry her books. Norma Jeane didn't understand what all the fuss was about. But she liked the attention.

One day a boy at school invited Norma Jeane for a date at the beach. She happily accepted. She had never been on a date before, and she had never seen the ocean "close-up."

As Norma Jeane strolled across the sand in a bathing suit borrowed from Bebe, she caught the attention of every boy on the beach. Flirtatious whistles rang out from all directions. Norma Jeane didn't seem to notice the ruckus she was causing—she was transfixed by the beauty of the Pacific Ocean. She took her date's hand and walked toward the lapping waves. The vast expanse of water gave her a powerful sensation. She felt happy and free.

"I paid no attention to the whistles and whoops," Marilyn recalled. "In fact, I didn't hear them. I was full of a strange feeling, as if I was two people. One of them was Norma Jeane from the orphanage who belonged to nobody. The other was someone whose name I didn't know. But I knew where she belonged. She belonged to the ocean and the sky and the whole world."

Norma Jeane as a teenager

CHILD BRIDE

ONE DAY IN THE SPRING OF 1941, NORMA JEANE AND
Bebe hurried on their way to school. A boy in a shiny
blue Ford coupe pulled up alongside the girls and offered
them a ride. Norma Jeane and Bebe recognized the boy.
His name was Jim Dougherty and he lived on their block.
Grace Goddard and the boy's mother, Ethel Dougherty,
were friends.

Grateful for the lift, Norma Jeane and Bebe hopped in
the car. Norma Jeane took note of Jim's broad shoulders,
thick brown hair, and mustache. She thought he was a
"dreamboat." Though he had graduated from high school
two years earlier, he still wore his varsity football jacket.
Confident and suave, Jim had been captain of the football
team and class president. Now he worked the night shift
at Lockheed Aircraft.

From that day forward, Jim gave Norma Jeane and Bebe
a ride to school every morning. Though Jim was four
years older than his two neighbors, he enjoyed their company. Over time, the three became friends. Jim was se-
cretly infatuated with fifteen-year-old Norma Jeane.

In early 1942, Doc Goddard made an announcement that would change many lives. He had been offered a good job in West Virginia. The whole family would be moving—the whole family except Norma Jeane. Although Grace and Doc were Norma Jeane's legal guardians, they couldn't adopt her without her mother's permission. Even though Gladys Baker had been institutionalized for years, she still had custody of Norma Jeane, and she refused to let the Goddards take her daughter away.

Grace felt that Aunt Ana was now too elderly to take responsibility for Norma Jeane. But Grace desperately wanted to avoid sending her back to the orphanage. Almost out of options, she came up with an idea. If Norma Jeane were to get married, Grace thought, the problem would be solved!

Matchmaker Grace quickly went to work. She figured her friend Ethel's handsome son Jim would be a good husband for Norma Jeane. She suggested the idea to Jim's parents. The Doughertys liked Norma Jeane. They thought she would be a loyal and caring wife for their son.

Ethel Dougherty approached her son. "The Goddards are going to West Virginia, and they're not taking Norma Jeane," she said. "She can't stay with Mrs. Lower, and that means she goes back to the orphanage until she's eighteen."

"I'm listening," Jim said.

"Grace wants to know if you'd be interested in marrying her."

Jim liked the idea, and so did Norma Jeane. A few months later, they announced their plan to marry.

With great enthusiasm, Aunt Ana entered the picture. She insisted on handling all the wedding arrangements. She painstakingly sewed a long white wedding gown for Norma Jeane. She notified out-of-town friends and relatives and suggested gifts appropriate for the young couple, such as pillowcases or table linens. She had elegant invitations printed:

> *Miss Ana Lower*
> *requests the honour of your presence*
> *at the marriage of her niece*
> *Norma Jean Baker*
> *to*
> *Mr. James E. Dougherty*
> *Friday, the nineteenth of June*
> *nineteen hundred and forty-two*
> *at 8:30 o'clock p.m.*
> *at the home of*
> *Mr. and Mrs. Chester Howell*
> *432 South Bentley Avenue*
> *Los Angeles, California*

Reception
Immediately after ceremony
432 South Bentley Avenue
Los Angeles, California

Norma Jeane Baker married Jim Dougherty on June 19, 1942, a couple of weeks after she turned "sweet sixteen."

Jim Dougherty

The wedding took place at the home of Chester Howell, an attorney friend of the Goddards. Norma Jeane descended the Howells' winding staircase with a bouquet of white carnations, her white veil flowing behind her. Unlike most brides, Norma Jeane had more than one set of parents at her wedding, including her foster parents Ida and Albert Bolender. The Goddards sent their best regards from West Virginia. Gladys Baker was unable to attend. Aunt Ana had the honor of giving the bride away.

Soon after the wedding, Norma Jeane and Jim moved into their first home, a one-room bungalow on Vista Del Monte in Sherman Oaks, California. Norma Jeane plunged into her new role as homemaker and wife. Unfortunately, she was hopeless as a housekeeper. One day she tried to dowse a small electrical fire with coffee grounds, and, in the process, spilled coffee over the entire carpet. Another time she tried to cook fish for dinner but forgot to turn the oven on. Quite often she prepared carrots and peas, because she liked the combination of colors.

Norma Jeane made an unusual bride. In many ways she was still a child. She enjoyed the company of children and surrounded herself with stuffed animals and dolls. Sometimes Norma Jeane sneaked out of the house to play games with the children in the neighborhood. Certainly, she was the only one on the block whose *husband* called her home when it began to get dark.

Over the next several months, Norma Jeane adjusted to married life. Jim gave her a dog to keep her company, a friendly collie she named Muggsy. Norma Jeane pampered Muggsy with fresh bones from the butcher and daily baths.

Norma Jeane also enjoyed doing special things for her husband. Every day when she packed his lunch for his graveyard shift at the factory, she would slip in a surprise love note: "When you read this, I'll be asleep and dreaming of you. Love and kisses, Your Baby."

Marriage meant something very important to Norma Jeane Dougherty. Being a married woman forever put to rest her status as "orphan."

THE MODEL

BY 1943 THE UNITED STATES WAS IN THE THICK OF
World War II. Underway since 1939, the complex and
bloody war involved many countries around the world
and had taken many lives. The United States had entered
the war in December 1941.

Many young men were drafted into the armed forces
during the war. Young Jim Dougherty knew that he would
eventually be drafted, so he decided to enlist in the Merchant Marine, a fleet of United States commercial ships.
Despite Norma Jeane's protest, Jim soon left for Catalina
Island, off the coast of Los Angeles. There he began basic
training to become a crew member on a trading ship.

The Merchant Marine made Jim a physical training in-
structor on the base. The on-base position meant a lot to
Jim. Norma Jeane could come and live with him on
Catalina Island. Jim hurried to a phone to call Norma
Jeane and tell her the good news that they would soon
be reunited. He later recalled that "she let out a shout
of joy you could have heard from North Hollywood to
Catalina without a phone."

The couple rented an apartment on Catalina. Some-times Norma Jeane, accompanied by Muggsy, would make the long walk to Jim's base. There she could watch Jim lead new recruits in rigorous exercises.

Norma Jeane always looked fresh and beautiful, no matter how hot a day it was. She like to wear lightweight clothing, such as a white blouse and slacks. Jim later wrote that Norma Jeane had "the cleanest kind of beauty I've ever seen. And she wore a ribbon in her hair quite of-ten, which added a touch of color."

The island surroundings were exotic and lush, but Jim and Norma Jeane could not ignore the reality of war. Jim was a Merchant Marine, a sailor, and sailors typically go to sea. Soon after Norma Jeane and Jim settled on Catalina, Jim made a heartbreaking announcement. He would soon be shipped out—to Townsville, Australia, on the other side of the planet.

The separation tore at Norma Jeane, who had been abandoned too many times in her young life. Reluctantly, she returned to Los Angeles and moved in with her mother-in-law, Ethel Dougherty.

Over the next year, Norma Jeane penned nearly two hundred love letters to Jim. Like many women and men at wartime, she was sad, lonely, and restless. Norma Jeane thought a job might take her mind off her worries. She asked Ethel Dougherty if there was a place for her at Radioplane, the factory in Burbank, California, where Ethel worked.

During World War II, many factories that manufactured

products like automobiles, aircraft, and household appliances joined in the defense effort. They produced military planes, helicopters, weapons, and supplies. Because of the great need for defense-related products, factory jobs were plentiful. Many men were away at war, however. Women were encouraged to join the workforce and take on the physically demanding factory jobs once allotted only to men.

Radioplane eagerly hired Norma Jeane. She started out on an assembly line with other women, spraying plastic "dope," or glue, on the outside of airplanes.The factory paid her thirty-three cents an hour for the work, the national minimum wage at the time.

Norma Jeane excelled as a sprayer—the factory even gave her an award. Still, the work was tedious. Norma Jeane was glad when she was transferred to another duty, inspecting and folding parachutes.

Though she handled factory work with skill and enthusiasm, Norma Jeane wasn't destined to spend the rest of her years working the assembly line. Lady Luck had different designs for the girl born in Hollywood.

One day an army photographer named David Conover visited Radioplane. Conover was on special assignment, under orders of his commanding officer, Captain Ronald Reagan, an actor and soldier who later became president of the United States. Conover was to photograph female factory workers participating in the war effort. The photographs would appear in *Yank,* a popular magazine for U.S. servicemen, and were intended as a "morale boost."

David Conover's photographs of Norma Jeane working at the aircraft factory were the first step to her modeling and film career.

It didn't take Conover long to notice Norma Jeane. He snapped several shots of her on the assembly line, dressed in the gray coveralls she wore on the job. He was impressed with her natural beauty and ease in front of the camera. After a while, Conover asked Norma Jeane if he could photograph her in her street clothes. She went to her locker and slipped on a pretty, apple-red sweater. As his camera clicked and flashed, Conover smiled. He had a feeling the pictures would be sensational.

An early modeling shot

Shortly after Conover's photo shoot at Radioplane, Norma Jeane received a brochure from Emmeline Snively, one of Hollywood's foremost modeling agents and owner of the Blue Book Agency. A photographer friend of Conover's had shown Emmeline the photos taken at the factory. Impressed, Emmeline wanted Norma Jeane to enroll in her modeling course.

Norma Jeane strolled into Emmeline's office wearing a shiny white "sharkskin" dress, her brownish-blonde hair just touching her shoulders. Emmeline appreciated Norma Jeane's natural, "girl-next-door" looks. She assured her she would have no trouble finding her modeling work. But Norma Jeane could not afford the school's tuition fee of one hundred dollars. Emmeline, confident in Norma Jeane's potential as a model, offered to cover her tuition with the money she would earn from her first modeling assignment.

Emmeline told Norma Jeane that the Holga Steel Company needed hostesses for an upcoming industrial show at the Pan-Pacific Auditorium. A hostess didn't need modeling experience, Emmeline said, she just needed to be pretty and personable. Later that day, Norma Jeane was hired as a hostess, or "floor model," for the convention. She would receive ten dollars a day for the ten day job, just enough to cover the cost of her tuition.

Soon Norma Jeane was one of Blue Book's most popular models. She got more hostess jobs and sometimes made as much as twenty-five dollars a day, a lot of money at the time. And because of her experience modeling for

Yank, she landed more magazine assignments. After a while, Norma Jeane was certain she could make a living from modeling, so she quit her job at Radioplane.

As if caught in a sudden cyclone, twenty-year-old Norma Jeane found that her life had changed radically in a few short months. As she thumbed through the stack of glossy magazines on her lap, her fingers trembled. Her face graced the cover of every magazine. Norma Jeane looked at her picture on the cover of *Yank.* She couldn't believe how attractive David Conover had made her look.

Conover's photographs launched Norma Jeane on a new career path. They also marked the beginning of her status as a "sex symbol." Although Norma Jeane had depth and intelligence, her physical beauty and her body were valued because of their appeal to men. She was often "objectified," or treated like an object rather than a complex human being. Her image became a symbol, and though her image was greatly admired, it had little to do with her true identity and inner spirit.

The abandoned orphan inside Norma Jeane—a sadness that would stay with her always—craved attention. Her role as a sex symbol gave her plenty of attention, but those who idolized her, her fans, didn't really know her and never would.

As a result, Norma Jeane, and later, Marilyn Monroe, often struggled with her identity—her sense of who she was. Attention from fans would never be enough for Marilyn Monroe. Because, too often, when her admirers weren't around, she would feel painfully alone once again.

★

As Norma Jeane became more and more focused on her career, her letters to Jim became infrequent. Their long-distance marriage began to suffer.

In early 1946 Jim came home for a brief leave. The war was over, but he was still serving in the Merchant Marine. At first Jim and Norma Jeane had a pleasant reunion. But then Norma Jeane began talking about her modeling career and her aspirations to become an actress. Jim disapproved—he wanted Norma Jeane to be a housewife, the typical and expected role for women at the time. He became annoyed with Norma Jeane's frequent departures to modeling jobs, which left him on his own.

One day Jim gave Norma Jeane an ultimatum. "You had better choose right now," he said. "Do you want to be Mrs. Jim Dougherty or a model?"

The silence he received was his answer. And in mid-May of 1946, Norma Jeane filed for divorce.

With Norma Jeane's new marital status came other changes. She moved into the Studio Club, an apartment complex managed by the wives of Hollywood executives. The Studio Club was a haven for young models and aspiring actresses, or "starlets."

Sometimes Norma Jeane felt lonely and homesick. She worried that she had made a mistake by divorcing Jim and quitting her job at the factory. Her thoughts sometimes turned to her mother. She had only seen Gladys a few

Many young starlets lived at the Studio Club in Hollywood.

times for short visits since Gladys was institutionalized. Norma Jeane's mother was practically a stranger to her.

Modeling jobs came only sporadically. Some weeks she had plenty of work, and at other times her phone didn't ring. When work was scarce, Norma Jeane skipped meals.

A modeling shot of Norma Jeane from 1946

"When you're young and healthy a little hunger isn't so important," she remembered. "What mattered more was being lonely. When you're young and healthy, loneliness can seem more important than it is."

With each new assignment, Norma Jeane grew more skilled and confident as a model. But Emmeline knew there was still much work to be done if Norma Jeane was going to make it in Hollywood.

One day Norma Jeane came to Emmeline in tears because a photographer had complained that her nose was too long. Emmeline carefully examined Norma Jeane's face. She told her there wasn't enough space between the end of her nose and her upper lip. She instructed Norma Jeane to pull her upper lip down when she smiled.

The new smile seemed ridiculous to Norma Jeane. But she knew that if she wanted to be a success in the modeling industry and in Hollywood, she would have to play by their rules. After many nights of practicing in front of a mirror, Norma Jeane mastered her new smile, though her lips always quivered with the effort.

Later, when Norma Jeane became famous, this self-conscious, awkward smile became one of her most memorable traits.

Emmeline encouraged Norma Jeane to lower her voice, and she showed her how to apply her makeup. Emmeline even tried to change the way Norma Jeane walked—which Emmeline considered "too wobbly." Emmeline said she "tried to correct that awful walk, but I couldn't. She had double-jointed knees."

Emmeline also encouraged Norma Jeane to change her hair color, because she often got requests for models with light blond hair. She secured an appointment for Norma Jeane at Frank and Joseph's, a first-rate Hollywood hair salon. Within hours, Norma Jeane was transformed. She stared at her new image in the salon mirror and smiled. She ran her fingers through the glamorous, wavy, golden blond hair that would become her trademark.

That night, the moon glowed and the stars sparkled over Hollywood. The "new" Norma Jeane dreamed about her future as she drove her battered old Ford coupe down Sunset Boulevard. The car, which she had shared with Jim, was her last tie to her ex-husband

HER NEW LIFE STRETCHED BEFORE HER, MYSTERIOUS AND BRIGHT LIKE THE HOLLYWOOD NIGHT.

and her former life. Her new life stretched before her, mysterious and bright like the Hollywood night.

"There must be thousands of girls sitting alone like me, dreaming of becoming a movie star," Norma Jeane thought as she turned onto Hollywood Boulevard.

"But I'm not going to worry about them. I'm dreaming the hardest."

CHAPTER SIX

MARILYN

"I WANT TO BE IN PICTURES," NORMA JEANE BOLDLY told Ben Lyon, head of new talent at Twentieth Century-Fox film studios on July 17, 1946. Though she was scared to death, she pretended that she wasn't.

Lyon looked at the twenty-year-old woman who stood in front of him. Lyon, who had "discovered" actress Jean Harlow several years earlier, was transfixed. Norma Jeane was the most beautiful woman he had ever seen. He knew she was going to be a movie star.

"Honey, you're in pictures!" Lyon said with a smile.

He told her he wanted to sign her to a seven-year contract, as long as she passed the screen test. Norma Jeane stared at Lyon in joyous disbelief. Her wish to be a movie actress was coming true, like a sweet dream unfolding before her eyes.

Lyon immediately took action. He called cameraman Leon Shamroy and director Walter Lang and asked them to shoot the screen test later that week. Then he scheduled appointments with a hairdresser and a makeup artist. He called the head of wardrobe at Fox and asked

Producer Ben Lyon and his wife, actress Bebe Daniels

him to select a beautiful gown for Norma Jeane to wear. Lyon wanted everything to be perfect.

At the appointed time, Norma Jeane stood in front of the camera in a sequined gown and high heels while Shamroy recorded one hundred feet of silent, Technicolor film.

"Walk across the set," he instructed. Norma Jeane teetered across the stage in her high heels.

"Sit down," he said. "Light a cigarette. Put it out. Go upstage. Cross. Look out a window. Sit down. Come downstage and exit."

Soon the screen test was over. Trembling, Norma Jeane went home. She had no idea if the studio would hire her. Nearly a week later, Lyon called her back into his office.

He announced that her screen test was sensational and offered her a contract. She would earn seventy-five dollars a week to start. Norma Jeane, overwhelmed with happiness, broke down and wept.

Later that day, Norma Jeane called Aunt Ana to share the good news. "It's the finest studio in the world," she told her. "The people are wonderful, and I'm going to be in a movie. It will be a small part. But once I'm on the screen . . . . "

A few days later, Lyon told Norma Jeane that her name would have to go. She needed a name that was more memorable and glamorous.

Lyon suggested "Carole Lind." Norma Jeane didn't like it. She wanted to use her grandmother's last name, Monroe. Lyon tried "Jean Monroe," but Norma Jeane didn't like that name either.

Lyon thought some more. Finally, he exclaimed, "I know who you are, you're Marilyn. I once knew a lovely actress named Marilyn, and you remind me of her." Norma Jeane nodded. She liked the name, too.

"Great!" Lyon said. "That has a nice flow, and two M's should be lucky."

Every morning, Marilyn Monroe roared through the gate at Fox Studios in her noisy old car—drawing quite a bit of attention to herself—just as her idol, Jean Harlow, had done a decade before. Unlike Harlow, however, Marilyn hadn't yet appeared in a film.

Marilyn tried to be patient as she waited to be called to her first film role. Meanwhile, she kept busy with the many classes required by the studio. Marilyn and the other stock actors practiced improvisation. They acted a skit or scene without any preparation, making it up as they went. Marilyn liked to improvise because she could be free and spontaneous, and she didn't have to remember any lines. She learned how to pantomime, or act using only gestures. She also took singing lessons and studied body movement and drama.

In 1947, nearly six months after being hired at Fox, Marilyn got her first film role. She would be an extra, an anonymous face in a crowd scene, in *Scudda-Hoo! Scudda-Hay!,* a romantic comedy about a farmer and a pair of mules. Marilyn knew the minor part could be her big break. Finally, she would be seen by the public and important people in the film industry.

Unfortunately, most of Marilyn's part, including her one line, "Hello," was cut from the film's final version. Only one shot of Marilyn survived, a long shot of her paddling a canoe on the far horizon of a lake.

In August 1947, Marilyn had her first speaking role. In her second film, *Dangerous Years,* she played a waitress in a jukebox joint for teenagers.

*Marilyn posed as a babysitter in an early publicity shot
for Twentieth Century-Fox.*

Just a few days after completing the film, Marilyn received an upsetting letter from the producers at Twentieth Century-Fox. They told her they did not wish to renew her contract. In short, Marilyn was fired, without explanation. Marilyn knew she wasn't yet a skilled actress. She needed more training, more time. Still, she felt angry at the studio for losing faith in her.

Marilyn applied for unemployment benefits. For months she lived on only thirty cents a day. To save

Marilyn had a small part in Dangerous Years *(1947).*

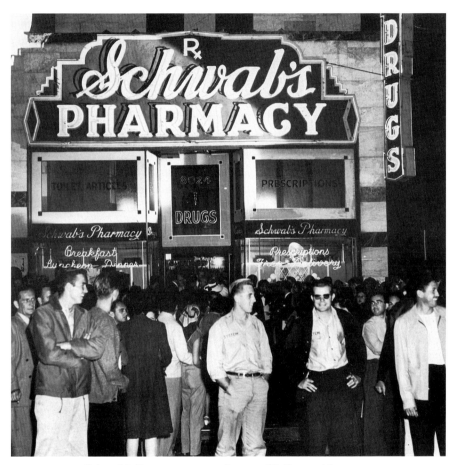

Schwab's Drugstore was a famous Hollywood hangout.

money, she ate simple meals, often only a hot dog or a sandwich, in her room at the Studio Club. She drank endless cups of coffee at Schwab's Drugstore on Sunset Boulevard, a hangout for struggling actors and artists.

There, Marilyn made friends who inspired her artistically and challenged her intellectually.

One of her new friends was Charlie Chaplin Jr., son of the silent film star of the 1920s. Like Marilyn, Charlie had experienced his share of hard luck. Charlie and Marilyn dated for a while. They remained good friends throughout their lives.

While unemployed, Marilyn educated herself. She opened a charge account at Marian Hunter's Bookshop and began a serious quest for knowledge. She fell in love with the writing of James Joyce, Ralph Waldo Emerson, and Walt Whitman. She liked poetry and biographies. She studied human anatomy and world history. Wherever she went, Marilyn usually had a book tucked under her arm.

One evening in early 1948, Joe Schenck, an executive at Fox Studios, invited Marilyn to dinner. Schenck, who had always liked Marilyn and hadn't been responsible for her being fired from Fox, wanted to help her.

"I think it's time you started making movies again," he said.

Marilyn gasped. "Do you mean it?"

"I sure do," he said.

Schenck called his old friend, Harry Cohn, who ran Columbia Studios. Within weeks, Marilyn had a new studio contract.

While Marilyn happily noted her turn of luck, she soon heard some sad news. In March 1948, Ana Lower passed away. Marilyn reflected on Aunt Ana's generosity toward her. Aunt Ana had given her unconditional love and guidance when she felt abandoned and lost. Her positive attitude and encouragement had boosted Norma Jeane's low self-esteem.

More than anything, Aunt Ana had taught Marilyn to have faith in herself. Because of Aunt Ana, Marilyn let herself dream.

AMERICA'S GREATEST MOVIE MAGAZINE

modern screen

DELL
MAGAZINE

MAR.
20c

Sidney Skolsky: THE LOWDOWN ON HOLLYWOOD WOMEN

Marilyn Monroe

STARDOM

"HELLO, I'M M...M...MARILYN."

The head drama coach at Columbia Studios, Natasha Lytess, stared at her new student in disbelief. Marilyn spoke in a high, breathy baby-voice and had a stunned look on her face. She wore a too-tight red dress. She walked stiffly and self-consciously.

Lytess, a former actress in Europe and a serious devotee of the acting craft, shook her head. Marilyn seemed too insecure to be a performer.

While doubtful at first, Lytess soon saw that Marilyn had talent. She also had *it*—the special, luminous quality that makes a star. Lytess was impressed with Marilyn's eagerness to learn, her genuineness, and her honesty. Marilyn was quick to admit her lack of skill, something most new actors would never do.

With Lytess's guidance, Marilyn learned how to relax and move freely. "These new sensations," Lytess remarked, "to a girl suffering from acute insecurity, were the difference between existing underwater and coming alive."

After several months of training, Marilyn took on her third film role with new confidence. In *Ladies of the Chorus,* she played Peggy, the daughter of a burlesque star who falls in love with a wealthy man. Marilyn danced and sang two songs for the role.

A reviewer from *Motion Picture Herald* wrote, "One of the bright spots is Miss Monroe's singing. She is pretty and, with her pleasing voice and style, she shows promise."

Marilyn was delighted. At last, a good review. But within days of completing the film, she received terrible

Marilyn (center, in black dress) was just another lady in Ladies of the Chorus *(1948).*

news. Her six-month contract at Columbia would not be renewed. Again she was fired without explanation.

Marilyn was discouraged, but she was not ready to give up. She struggled to make a living. She landed occasional modeling jobs, and for a while she worked as a magician's assistant.

In the spring of 1949, Marilyn sat on her favorite stool at Schwab's Drugstore and ate lunch. As she sipped a Coca-Cola, she overheard a conversation. The man seated next to her told his friend that the director of the new Marx Brothers film, *Love Happy,* was looking for an actress. He added that the part was small—the actress merely had to walk across the stage.

Marilyn was intrigued. She boldly asked the man for the audition address. She jumped off her stool and practically ran out of Schwab's. A million thoughts ran through her mind. What dress should she wear to the audition? What audition piece should she read? Later that day, Marilyn appeared on the set of *Love Happy* for her audition. Nervous and excited, she shook hands with the film's director, David Miller. Miller introduced Marilyn to Groucho and Harpo Marx, the famous comedian brothers.

"Can you walk?" Groucho asked Marilyn.

"I learned to walk when I was a baby, and I haven't had a lesson since," Marilyn answered matter-of-factly.

She strolled across the film set to prove herself. Groucho's eyes bugged out and he lifted his eyebrows up and down. Marilyn landed the part. It was a small, cameo role, but one that stood out in the film.

Marilyn starred with Groucho Marx in the 1949 movie Love Happy.

The producers of *Love Happy* sent Marilyn on a tour to promote the film. Billed as the "Mmm Girl" and the "Woo Woo Girl," Marilyn made guest appearances across the country. The film gained plenty of publicity—and so did Marilyn. Important people in the movie business started to talk about her. Marilyn's name and picture popped up in movie magazines such as *Photoplay*.

The entertainment business is unpredictable. One moment a person could be the hottest star in Hollywood, the

Marilyn turned to drama coach Natasha Lytess for inspiration and training.

next, an out-of-work actor. Fortunately for Marilyn, the same thing could happen in reverse. Though she had been recently unemployed, she was now in demand. Ironically, Twentieth Century-Fox, the first studio to fire her, wanted her back. And they were prepared to pay the price. Fox offered Marilyn five hundred dollars a week and her first serious screen role, in director John Huston's *The Asphalt Jungle.* Marilyn wasn't about to pass up the offer.

Marilyn hired her former drama coach, Natasha Lytess,

to help her prepare for her role as the girlfriend of an aging jewel thief.

On the first day of filming, Marilyn arrived on the set with shaky knees and butterflies in her stomach. She confessed her nervousness to director Huston.

"If you're *not* nervous, you might as well give up!" he replied. Then Huston flashed Marilyn a friendly smile.

Although she was terrified at first, Marilyn gave a strong performance. She received good reviews for her work in the film, which was a box-office success. Even Marilyn, who was her own toughest critic, later called her work in *The Asphalt Jungle* her finest.

Director Huston was especially impressed. "She went right down into her own personal experience for everything, reached down and pulled something out of herself that was unique and extraordinary," he said. "She had no techniques. It was all the truth, it was only Marilyn."

> SHE HAD NO TECHNIQUES. IT WAS ALL THE TRUTH, IT WAS ONLY MARILYN.

Other directors soon asked to work with Marilyn. Joseph L. Mankiewicz directed her next Fox film, *All About Eve,* the story of a stage actress's vicious climb to Broadway stardom. The film featured an all-star cast, led by Bette Davis. Marilyn played Miss Caswell, a graduate of "The Cocacabana School of Dramatic Art."

Although Marilyn's role was minor, critics praised her performance. *All About Eve* won several Academy Awards for 1950, including the Oscar for Best Picture.

As her popularity increased, so did her salary. Marilyn soon netted $750 a week at Fox. She appeared in several films in the following months, including *Home Town Story, As Young As You Feel,* and *Love Nest.* In the 1951 comedy *Let's Make It Legal,* Marilyn played a gold digger who husband-hunts at a fancy hotel. Though the film was forgettable, Marilyn created her own memorable "scenes" during the film's shooting.

Marilyn often arrived late on the set, keeping the film's stars, Claudette Colbert and Macdonald Carey, waiting. Director Richard Sale quickly tired of her tardiness. One day when Marilyn arrived forty minutes late, Sale screamed at her in front of the entire cast and crew and demanded an apology. Marilyn refused and stomped away, only to return a few minutes later to apologize to everyone. She even gave director Sale a hug. She really was sorry about her lateness. She just couldn't help it.

Marilyn's habitual tardiness soon became the talk of the town. Not only was Marilyn usually late to work, she was late to appointments, dates, and public speaking engagements. Once Marilyn missed a plane because she stopped in the boarding gate to put on a little more lipstick. She was even late for her own appendectomy!

Marilyn had a simple explanation for her lateness: "It's not really me that's late," she said. "It's the others who are in such a hurry."

Some writers believe that Marilyn's insecurity caused her chronic lateness. In the mid-1950s, a writer for *Time* magazine reported, "The truth is that Marilyn has been so

terrified of failure during most of her life that she has often had to screw up her courage for the slightest en-
counter with the world.

"Before the least important interview she will put on
her make-up five or six times before she is satisfied with
her looks."

For the most part, directors and coworkers tolerated
Marilyn's lateness. They knew that Marilyn was a box-
office draw—her electric screen presence made up for her
bad habits.

In the 1952 movie *Clash by Night,* Marilyn received
costar billing with Barbara Stanwyck and received favor-
able reviews for her performance as a blue-jean-clad fish
cannery worker.

Marilyn played opposite stars Cary Grant and Ginger
Rogers in her next film, the madcap comedy *Monkey
Business.* The film featured Marilyn as a secretary named
Lois Laurel, a real chimpanzee, and a zany plot about a
magic youth potion.

In *Niagara,* Marilyn took on a more serious role, as a
scheming, dangerous woman staying at a honeymoon va-
cation lodge. The film was shot on location at Niagara
Falls in New York state. A reviewer wrote of Marilyn in
Niagara, "She is unearthly *striking* . . . everyone and
everything, including the falls, is secondary to Marilyn
Monroe's presence."

In one scene, Marilyn walks away from the camera for a
very long time. The audience watches as Marilyn, dressed
in a black skirt and bright red blouse and wobbling on

The famous "Diamonds Are a Girl's Best Friend" number from Gentlemen Prefer Blondes *(1953)*.

high heels, fades into the distance. The 116-foot walk was, at the time, the longest on-screen walk in film history.

Marilyn took the lead as Loralei Lee in the musical comedy *Gentlemen Prefer Blondes,* released in 1953. Before filming began, she rehearsed each song and dance number over and over again. She wanted her performance to be perfect.

Marilyn's hard work showed in the film. In one of Marilyn's most famous scenes, she danced down a staircase and sang "Diamonds Are a Girl's Best Friend." She had to perform the difficult routine in an uncomfortably tight evening gown and high heels. Though the performance was difficult, Marilyn made it look easy.

One writer seemed more impressed by Marilyn's vibrant good looks than her work in the film. "Miss Monroe looks as though she would glow in the dark," wrote a critic from the *New York Herald Tribune.*

In the summer of 1953, Marilyn and her *Gentlemen Prefer Blondes* costar, Jane Russell, placed their handprints and autographs in wet cement outside Grauman's Chinese Theatre on Hollywood Boulevard. Traditionally, only stars who had officially "made it" were honored in the cement yard of the theater. After Marilyn signed her name, she dotted the "i" in Marilyn with a rhinestone—to commemorate the song "Diamond's Are a Girl's Best Friend." (Soon afterward, a souvenir-hunting thief stole the rhinestone.)

Fame came as a surprise to Marilyn. In many ways, she still felt like Norma Jeane, the quiet, simple girl she used to be. But now she was a celebrity and a sex symbol. Everyone treated her differently. "I feel as though it's all happening to someone right next to me," Marilyn said of her stardom. "I'm close, I can feel it, I can hear it, but it isn't really me."

Marilyn showed her flair for comedy in *How To Marry a Millionaire,* which also starred Lauren Bacall and Betty

Marilyn and Jane Russell kicked up their heels in
Gentlemen Prefer Blondes.

Grable. "Her stint as a dead-pan comedienne is as nifty as her looks," wrote Otis Guernsey Jr. in the New York *Herald Tribune*. "Playing a near-sighted charmer who won't wear her glasses when men are around, she bumps into the furniture and reads books upside down."

The film helped earn Marilyn the 1953 Photoplay Award as the most popular actress in Hollywood. That year Marilyn earned more money for her studio than any other actress.

Marilyn and costar Jane Russell place their handprints in the cement in Hollywood's "Walk of Fame."

Marilyn performs a glamorous dance number in How to Marry
a Millionaire *(1953).*

While Marilyn kept busy professionally, she also had a
full social life. She loved to dress up and go out on the
town. Many men wanted to date Marilyn. She had plenty
of boyfriends, but to her disappointment, none of her re-
lationships lasted.

Meanwhile, one very famous man had taken a special
interest in Marilyn—but she hadn't met him yet. He was
considered one of the greatest baseball players of all time.
His name was Joe DiMaggio.

Marilyn Monroe married baseball great Joe DiMaggio in 1954.

New Directions

"I DON'T CARE TO MEET HIM," MARILYN TOLD talent agent David March in the spring of 1952. "I don't like men in loud clothes, with checked suits and big muscles and pink ties. I get nervous."

March assured Marilyn that his friend—baseball great Joe DiMaggio—was not the sort of man she was expecting.

Months earlier, Joe DiMaggio had spotted Marilyn in a sports magazine, posing for a publicity shot with the Chicago White Sox baseball team. One look at Marilyn, with a baseball bat and a big smile, was enough for Joe. He called a few friends in the entertainment business, attempting to find someone who knew Marilyn. Finally, Joe talked to his friend David March.

March had worked with Marilyn and knew her well. On a personal level, he thought Joe and Marilyn would make a nice couple. Professionally, he knew the pairing of the baseball hero and the movie star would make great publicity.

After much encouragement, Marilyn agreed to meet
Joe, who was in town on business. David March and his
girlfriend would also come along. Marilyn agreed to ren-
dezvous with the group at six-thirty the next evening.

The next night Joe DiMaggio sat with his friends in the
Villa Nova, a popular Italian restaurant on Sunset Boulevard in Hollywood, waiting for his date to arrive. He
craned his neck in all directions. He looked at his watch.
Already a half-hour late, Marilyn was nowhere in sight.

Joe started to worry. Had Marilyn stood him up?

March tried to reassure Joe. "Haven't you heard? Marilyn
Monroe is always late!"

Nearly two hours later, diners at the Villa Nova stared
in surprise as Marilyn Monroe strolled into the restaurant. She looked beautiful in a simple cocktail dress. Joe's
eyes lit up when he spotted her.

"Sorry I'm late," she said, smiling at Joe. She shook his
hand and looked him over. March was right. Joe wasn't at
all like she expected him to be.

Joseph Paul DiMaggio, a tall man of Italian descent,
was thirty-seven years old—twelve years older than
Marilyn. He had graying hair and looked businesslike in
a dark suit. His years of playing baseball for the New York
Yankees showed on his muscular build, but he wasn't
like other famous athletes Marilyn had met. Joe was
quiet, shy, and reserved. Marilyn tried to make Joe smile.
"There's a blue polka dot exactly in the middle of your tie
knot," she said. "Did it take you long to fix it like that?"
Joe shook his head "no."

Joe DiMaggio played outfield for the New York Yankees from 1936 to 1951. By the time he met Marilyn, he'd retired from professional baseball, but to the American public he was still a hero.

As they ate anchovies on pimiento peppers, spaghetti, and scallopini of veal, Joe and Marilyn hardly said a word to one another, but they enjoyed each other's company. "He didn't try to impress me or anybody else," Marilyn wrote of the meeting. "Mr. DiMaggio just sat there. Yet somehow he was the most exciting man at the table. The excitement was in his eyes. They were sharp and alert."

The next day Marilyn told her friends about the "marvelous man" she had met. She was going out with him again that night.

Marilyn dated Joe every night until he returned to New York two weeks later. After that, she kept in touch with him by phone. The gossip columns buzzed with news of their relationship. Rumors circulated about a possible marriage. Marilyn would only comment to the press, "I want to love and be loved more than anything in the world."

Meanwhile, Marilyn's career kept her busy. She made headlines during the filming of *River of No Return*. The movie, costarring Robert Mitchum, was filmed in the Canadian Rocky Mountains and featured dramatic footage of river rafting. During one shoot, Marilyn tripped and fell into the river, and her high rubber waders filled with water. The crew swiftly rescued Marilyn from the racing river. The next day headlines across the country read, "MARILYN MONROE NEARLY DROWNED."

Though the film had some exciting moments, Marilyn felt disappointed. The movie, which flopped at the box office, was not up to her standards. She was getting tired of roles that were not challenging or serious. Often cast as the "dumb blonde" or the "love interest," Marilyn felt that the producers at Twentieth Century-Fox did not appreciate her acting skills. They did not give her any choice about what parts she played.

During production of her next film, a lighthearted comedy called *Pink Tights*, Marilyn reached her breaking point. "I read the script and didn't like it," she said. "The part isn't right for me. It's as simple as that." Defiantly, she did not show up on the set for work on the film.

Joe sympathized with her. He presented her with an idea: "You're having all this trouble with the studio . . . Why don't we get married now? I've got to go to Japan on some baseball business, and we could make a honeymoon out of the trip."

On January 14, 1954, Marilyn wed Joe DiMaggio at the San Francisco City Hall. Instead of a gown, Marilyn wore a tailored brown suit with a fur collar. Joe, also in a suit, gave Marilyn a white-gold ring with a circle of diamonds.

Marilyn and Joe were all smiles on their wedding day, January 14, 1954.

Marilyn was more than happy to disappear from Hollywood for a while. She looked forward to being an ordinary, anonymous person in Japan.

Marilyn was in for a surprise. When she and Joe arrived in Japan, they were shocked to see huge crowds gathered at the airport. Thousands of fans hoped to catch a glimpse of Marilyn and her new husband. They overturned cars and smashed windows. Many yelled, "*Man-chan, Man-chan,*" which means "Sweet Little Girl" in Japanese. Some frenzied fans ripped out strands of Marilyn's hair.

When newlyweds Joe and Marilyn got off the plane in Tokyo, they were mobbed by fans, members of the press, and photographers.

Marilyn took time out from her honeymoon to perform for American troops in Seoul, Korea, in 1954.

While Marilyn incited near-riots, Joe launched the 1954 Japanese baseball season. Two years earlier, Joe had played his last competitive baseball game in Tokyo. Now he was one of the most well-loved Americans in Japan.

Marilyn interrupted her honeymoon for a four-day trip to Korea, to perform for the American troops in Seoul, fighting in the Korean War. Seventeen thousand soldiers went wild when Marilyn, dressed only in a purple evening gown, stood in a snowstorm and sang to them. "I felt as warm as if I were standing in a bright sun," Marilyn said. "I felt for the first time in my life no fear of anything."

When the newlyweds returned to the States, Joe had a serious talk with Marilyn. He told her he hated her Hollywood image. And he didn't like the idea of millions of men being in love with his wife. Joe, like Marilyn's first husband, wanted her to quit her job and be a housewife.

In the 1950s, a woman's social role was narrowly defined. Typically, married women were expected to work at home raising children, cooking, and cleaning, while their husbands worked outside the home. Marilyn had a hard time living up to Joe's, and society's, expectations of her. After nearly six months away from the bright lights of Hollywood, Marilyn decided she wasn't ready to give up her career. Despite Joe's protests, Marilyn went back to work.

After playing a small part in the musical *There's No Business Like Show Business,* Marilyn was cast as a lead in the comedy *The Seven Year Itch,* directed by Billy Wilder. She played a woman who tries to win the affection of her married downstairs neighbor.

One particular scene in the film, shot in September 1954 in New York City, was to become Marilyn's most famous moment on screen.

In the scene, Marilyn stood on a sidewalk grating as a draft from the subway below blew her white skirt up and over her head. Though the scene was shot at two o'clock in the morning, more than two thousand onlookers gathered to view the spectacle.

The infamous "skirt scene" from The Seven Year Itch.

Unfortunately, one of those who saw the "skirt scene" was Marilyn's husband, who had dropped by to watch the shoot.

"What's going on here?" Joe yelled. He watched as the crowd screamed each time Marilyn's skirt blew in the air. Joe was furious. He didn't want to share Marilyn with the world.

Marilyn and Joe could not resolve their differences. In October 1954 Marilyn told director Wilder that she and Joe

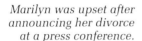

Marilyn was upset after announcing her divorce at a press conference.

were going to divorce. By November the divorce was final.

Marilyn hardly had time to grieve her loss. She had too much work to do. Some days she was expected to put in as many as eighteen hours on the movie set. Meanwhile, she had developed a dangerous habit.

In the "golden" era of Hollywood, from the silent movie days of the 1920s up through the 1950s, many stars developed a serious dependency on drugs—especially legal, doctor-prescribed medication. The studio physician commonly dispensed "uppers" (amphetamines) to actors to give them the extra energy they needed to make it through a long workday. Just as often, the doctor also prescribed "downers"—barbituates—to help the actors sleep at night. Drug use was considered ordinary and was even encouraged.

DESPITE HER PHENOMENAL SUCCESS IN HOLLYWOOD, MARILYN WASN'T VERY HAPPY.

Certainly, not all actors became dependent on drugs, but Marilyn did. She also began to drink heavily, especially champagne. Her bad habits took a serious toll on her physical and mental health.

In November, Marilyn's friends decided to cheer her up. They threw her a big party at Romanoff's restaurant in Beverly Hills to celebrate the completion of *The Seven Year Itch*. The brightest stars in Hollywood were invited, including Humphrey Bogart, Lauren Bacall, Gary Cooper, Doris Day, and even Marilyn's childhood idol, Clark Gable.

That night Marilyn stared at her guests with wonder. "I feel like Cinderella," she told a friend. "I didn't think they'd all show up. Honest."

Despite her phenomenal success in Hollywood, Marilyn wasn't very happy. Her marriage to Joe had ended in failure, in large part because he could not accept her acting career. But she still wasn't getting the kind of roles she wanted, and the pressures and demands of being a celebrity had started to weigh on her. "Everybody is always tugging at you," she wrote in her autobiography. "They'd all like . . . a chunk of you. They . . . take pieces out of you."

Marilyn knew she needed a break from Hollywood. She wanted some time just for herself.

In late December, Marilyn, calling herself "Zelda Zonk," put on a black wig and dark glasses and boarded a plane for New York City.

For once, no one begged for her autograph.

Many of the biggest stars in Hollywood, including Lauren Bacall and Humphrey Bogart, gathered at a party to lift Marilyn's spirits.

Marilyn was surrounded by reporters at a press conference at which she announced her divorce. The more famous Marilyn became, the less privacy she had. Reporters noted her every move.

NEW YORK AND BEYOND

IN THE 1950S, NEW YORK'S ACTORS STUDIO WAS known as the best acting school in the country. The school, founded by Lee Strasberg, introduced the Method, an acting style that encourages actors to draw on their own emotions and experience. Many talented actors received their early training at the Actors Studio, including Marlon Brando, James Dean, Jane Fonda, Sally Field, and Paul Newman. The Method technique is still widely used.

In January 1955 Marilyn surprised many people in Hollywood. She announced that she wished to study at the Actors Studio. "I want to be a real actress," she told the press.

Marilyn asked Lee Strasberg if she could enroll in his school. Strasberg, a tough teacher who had rejected such future stars as Jack Nicholson and Barbra Streisand from his school, wholeheartedly accepted Marilyn.

"I saw that what she looked like was not what she really was," Strasberg said. "And what was going on inside was not what was going on outside, and that always means there may be something there to work with."

Strasberg took Marilyn under his wing. For a time he gave her free private classes in his home. He introduced Marilyn to his wife, Paula, an acting coach, and his teenage daughter, Susan, an aspiring actress. The Strasbergs soon "adopted" Marilyn, who craved and adored being part of a family. After her acting lessons, Marilyn usually stayed for dinner. She loved the simple meals that Paula prepared, such as red cabbage and brisket, or tender pot roast simmered with potatoes and onions.

Susan especially liked Marilyn. Though Marilyn was a movie star, she talked easily about ordinary things like books, boys, and clothes. "I forgot she was almost thirty years old," Susan recalled later. "She seemed like one of my girlfriends, maybe a little more fun, a little freer, and much more interesting."

Once Marilyn told Susan how much she appreciated Lee as a teacher. "With your father . . . I feel it's okay to be me," she explained. "The whole kit and caboodle, you know, the whole mess."

Under the Strasberg influence, Marilyn grew happier and more confident. She painted watercolors and wrote poetry. And, to Marilyn's delight, her acting improved.

Marilyn usually came to class at the Actors Studio dressed in a baggy sweater, jeans, and no makeup. She always sat in the back of the room. Marilyn wanted to be

Susan Strasberg

treated just like a regular student. She didn't take advantage of her fame.

In New York, Marilyn enjoyed the company of other serious artists. The Strasbergs introduced her to poets Carl Sandburg and Edith Sitwell. She hit it off with author Truman Capote.

At dinner one evening, Paula Strasberg told Marilyn she had a friend who wanted to meet her. Would Marilyn meet him for lunch the next day? While she was usually unenthusiastic about blind dates, this time Marilyn was delighted. Arthur Miller was a Pulitzer Prize-winning playwright, author of such plays as *Death of a Salesman, The Crucible,* and *All My Sons.* Marilyn had admired his writing for years.

The next day, Marilyn sat on a couch at the Strasberg home next to Arthur Miller. At thirty-nine, Arthur was tall, lean, and quiet. Marilyn thought he looked a lot like Abraham Lincoln, who was one of her heroes. Though Marilyn and Arthur couldn't find much to talk about, they had a wonderful time.

Marilyn and Arthur dated regularly for months. They usually met in private, out-of-the-way restaurants to avoid the press and photographers. They both knew they were falling in love, but they weren't ready to tell the world about it.

In December Marilyn decided she was ready for a big career change. With newfound confidence, she formed her own film production company, Marilyn Monroe Productions, with her friend Milton Greene. She now had greater control over her acting future.

Marilyn Monroe Productions soon negotiated a deal with Twentieth Century-Fox. Fox was eager to sign Marilyn to a new contract, but she insisted on some major changes. She wanted $100,000 per film—significantly more than the weekly salary Fox had paid her as a stock player. Also, she demanded approval of all her future movie scripts.

In February 1956 Marilyn flew back to Los Angeles. On the plane she wondered if her fans had forgotten her while she was away in New York. She soon had her answer. Hundreds of men, women, and children greeted Marilyn at the airport. The crowd was so thick that she couldn't leave the airport for over two hours.

Arthur Miller and Marilyn Monroe

Marilyn eagerly started work on her first film under the new contract, *Bus Stop*, which was adapted from a Broadway play. In *Bus Stop,* Marilyn played Cherie, a saloon singer who is "roped in" by a wife-hunting rodeo cowboy, played by Don Murray.

Paula Strasberg came to Hollywood to coach Marilyn in the film. In *Bus Stop,* Marilyn used the Method technique of acting she had learned in New York. Many critics felt that Marilyn did her finest work in this film. The *Herald Tribune* reported, "In *Bus Stop* she has a wonderful role, and she plays it with a mixture of humor and pain that is very touching."

A critic from *The New York Times* was even more exuberant. "Hold onto your chairs, everybody, and get set for a rattling surprise," he wrote. "Marilyn Monroe has finally proved herself an actress in *Bus Stop.* She and the picture are swell!!"

Soon, in June 1956, Marilyn made worldwide headlines again, but not for a part she was playing in a film. At a New York press conference, Marilyn and Arthur broke their secret to the world. They were not only in love, they were getting married.

On June 29, Marilyn Monroe became, legally, Marilyn Miller—coincidentally, the same name as the actress who had inspired her first name. Arthur gave Marilyn a gold ring inscribed "A. to M., June 1956. Now is forever." Marilyn wrote her sentiments on the back of their wedding photograph: "Hope. Hope. Hope."

Marilyn and Arthur didn't have time for a honeymoon.

Arthur and Marilyn were married on June 29, 1956.

Instead, they flew to England for the production of Marilyn's next film. Marilyn costarred with the renowned British actor Sir Laurence Olivier in *The Prince and the Showgirl.* Marilyn was at first excited to work with Olivier. She affectionately called him "Larry," and he called her "Sweetie." But by production's end, Olivier and Marilyn were hardly speaking.

Marilyn had to pretend she enjoyed flirting with Laurence Olivier, whom she disliked.

Olivier despised Marilyn's lateness. And, as a classically-trained actor, he didn't approve of her Method acting technique. Marilyn also grew to dislike Olivier. "He gave me the dirtiest looks, even when he was smiling," she remembered.

In one scene in the movie, Marilyn's acting skills were challenged. She had to flirt with Olivier, a man she didn't like. "Think of Frank Sinatra and Coca-Cola," advised acting coach Paula Strasberg. With her favorite singer and soda in mind, Marilyn acted convincingly in the scene.

Marilyn's next film, a comedy called *Some Like It Hot,* was a greater success. Marilyn played a ukulele player in a jazz band. Costars Jack Lemmon and Tony Curtis played crook musicians who disguise themselves as women so they can be a part of the all-female band.

In 1959 *Some Like It Hot* was the most successful comedy in the history of motion pictures. That year Marilyn won a Golden Globe Award for best actress in a comedy or musical. Marilyn herself was less than thrilled with the film, however. It disturbed her that she had been, once again, cast as a "dumb blonde." "Dumb enough," she remarked, "to believe those guys [Lemmon's and Curtis's characters] were girls."

"Why do I have to act dumb?" complained Marilyn. "Can't I do something else? Anything?"

Despite her efforts to be taken seriously as an actress, she was repeatedly cast as a one-dimensional woman. Audiences adored her because she was beautiful and sexy, and movie producers knew that sexiness would

Although Some Like It Hot *was a big hit, Marilyn complained about being cast once again as a "dumb blonde."*

sell. Feminist Gloria Steinem said of Marilyn, "She lived in a time when her body was far more rewarded that the spirit inside. Her body became her prison."

In many of her films, Marilyn played a naive, not-so-bright character. Marilyn's fans rarely saw her deeper self. Often Marilyn felt lonely, because most people didn't know who she really was. She struggled to understand her true self. She numbed herself with champagne and the prescription drugs she thought she couldn't live without.

Marilyn had become so famous she couldn't live a normal life. She couldn't do even the simplest thing, like go to the corner store for a carton of milk, without drawing a crowd or being chased. Because of this, Marilyn spent much of her time alone.

Photographers wait outside Marilyn and Arthur's home in Connecticut, hoping to catch her.

■

THE FINAL CHAPTER

MARILYN AND ARTHUR SHARED AN APARTMENT on Fifty-seventh Street in New York City, but Marilyn rarely saw her husband. Arthur spent much of his time writing in his study. He rarely even joined Marilyn for meals. Marilyn worried that her marriage to Arthur was falling apart.

Arthur didn't like to go out to dinner or nightclubs with Marilyn. To entertain herself, Marilyn talked on the phone to friends. She also liked to eat meals in bed. "She liked Italian food," said Marilyn's housekeeper, Lena Pepitone. "In fact, she *loved* it. My cooking became a highlight in her life: spaghetti, lasagna, sausages, and peppers were treats to her, just as candy and soda pop are to little children."

Loneliness and Lena's cooking had a predictable effect on Marilyn. She gained weight. By the time she flew to Reno, Nevada, to shoot her twenty-ninth motion picture,

The Misfits, in July 1960, Marilyn had put on over twenty pounds.

The Misfits had special importance to Marilyn. Arthur Miller wrote the film's screenplay as a gift to her. Years ahead of its time, the film dealt with the issue of animal rights. The cause was important to Marilyn.

Clark Gable, her lifelong idol, was her costar. The film also starred Marilyn's good friend Montgomery Clift. Shot

Director John Huston, Marilyn, and Arthur Miller on the set of The Misfits.

in black-and-white film and featuring the vast, dry land-scape of the Nevada desert, *The Misfits* was a departure from the lighthearted musicals and comedies that Marilyn had made in the past. Finally, she was working on a film that mattered to her.

In *The Misfits* Marilyn played Roslyn, a lonely woman who goes to Reno to seek a divorce. She soon meets Gay (played by Gable), a rugged cowboy whose job is to round up wild horses to be sold for dog food. Roslyn, who falls in love with Gay, desperately struggles to save the wild horses from destruction.

Though the film had all the makings of a success, the production proved to be a disaster. Each day, the temperature climbed near 110 degrees. The cast and crew were miserable in the desert heat.

The heat especially affected Marilyn. She couldn't sleep at night and had trouble staying awake during the day. The medication she took made her groggy. Tempers blazed as Marilyn, appearing tired and dazed, arrived late on the set every day. In August, Marilyn reached her physical and emotional limits. She spent a week in Westwood Hospital in Los Angeles to recover from exhaustion.

After a week's rest, Marilyn returned to Reno to complete *The Misfits*. Though under stress, Marilyn and her costars gave powerful performances. Paul Beckley of the New York *Herald Tribune* wrote, "There are lines one feels Miss Monroe must have said on her own . . . And can anyone deny that in this film these performers are at their best?"

Marilyn got to work with her idol Clark Gable in The Misfits. *Sadly, it was the actor's last film; he died shortly after it was completed.*

Clark Gable considered his work in the film one of his best performances. "Gable's acting is vibrant and lusty," wrote critic Kate Cameron of the New York *Daily News.* Sadly, Clark Gable did not live to see the finished film. A week after filming was completed, he died of a heart attack, on November 16, 1960. Marilyn blamed herself. She felt that Gable's heart attack was brought on by stress endured while working with her on *The Misfits.*

While Marilyn grieved the death of Gable, she faced an-other ending. Her marriage to Arthur, rocky for months, was coming to a close. In January 1961, Marilyn and Arthur were divorced, after more than four years of marriage.

"I still don't understand it," Arthur said to a friend a week after the divorce. "We got through it. I made a pres-ent of this *[The Misfits]* to her, and I left it without her."

After the divorce, Marilyn tried to put her life back to-gether. She told the *Los Angeles Times,* "I am trying to find myself as a person. Millions of people live their en-tire lives without finding themselves . . . "

Marilyn's good friends offered their support. Popular singer Frank Sinatra cheered her up with a little white poodle. She named the dog "Maf." Joe DiMaggio, who still loved Marilyn, visited her often. He and Marilyn al-ways remained friends.

In the spring of 1962 Marilyn started work on *Some-thing's Got To Give,* a comedy about a woman who is pre-sumed dead for years and reappears on the day her husband is to remarry. As a publicity stunt for the film, Marilyn was asked to sing to President John F. Kennedy at his birthday celebration in New York City.

Marilyn wanted to look spectacular for the occasion. She had a special gown sewn of thin, white cloth embroi-dered with rhinestones. At five thousand dollars, the gown was the most expensive item of clothing Marilyn had ever purchased.

On the evening of her performance, Marilyn stood in front of a crowd of fifteen thousand people in Madison

Square Garden. Her beautiful gown sparkled in the spot-
light. Marilyn was nervous. In a voice soft as a whisper,
she began to sing for the President:

Happy—birthday—to you,
Happy birthday to you,
Happy birthday Mr. Pres—i—dent,
Happy birthday to you....

The crowd applauded wildly as Marilyn walked off the
stage. Then President Kennedy walked up to the micro-
phone. "Thank you," he said. "I can now retire from pol-
itics after having had 'Happy Birthday' sung to me in
such a sweet, wholesome way."

The birthday tribute stands as a golden, glistening moment in Marilyn's life.

*One of the most memorable moments in Marilyn's life was when
she sang Happy Birthday to President John F. Kennedy in 1962.*

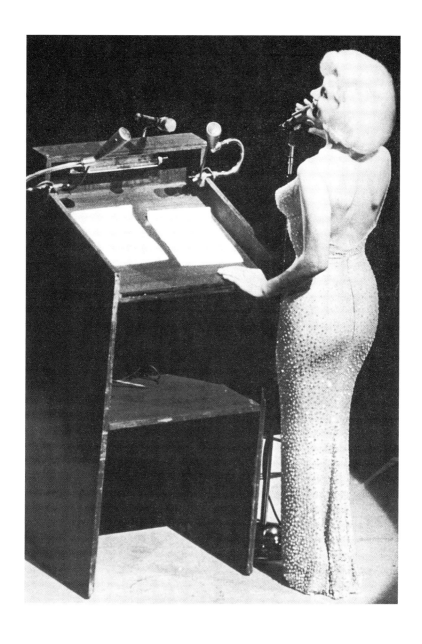

EPILOGUE

ON SUNDAY, AUGUST 5, 1962, MARILYN MONROE was found dead in her Los Angeles home at the age of thirty-six. She had died of an overdose of sleeping pills. Though her death appeared to be a suicide, some people believe that Marilyn did not take her own life. In many ways, the circumstances surrounding her death are clouded in mystery.

Joe DiMaggio handled Marilyn's funeral arrangements. He insisted that Marilyn have a private, peaceful funeral, "so that she can go to her final resting place in the quiet she always sought."

On August 7, a recording of "Over the Rainbow," sung by Judy Garland, floated through the tiny chapel at Westwood Village Mortuary in Hollywood. Marilyn, in a simple green dress, appeared to be asleep in her casket. Twenty-five mourners, including Marilyn's half-sister, Berniece, gathered to say good-bye to Marilyn.

Lee Strasberg wept as he said Marilyn's eulogy: "She had a luminous quality, a combination of wistfulness, radiance, yearning—that set her apart and yet made everyone wish to be part of it, to share in the childish naiveté which was at once so shy and yet so vibrant."

As the service came to a close, Joe DiMaggio placed a small bouquet of pink roses in Marilyn's clasped hands. He kissed her one last time and whispered, "I love you, I love you, I love you."

Many people loved Marilyn in her lifetime. And, more than thirty years after her death, she is still loved. Her legacy, her work in film, endures. Marilyn will be making people laugh and cry for generations to come.

Pop star Madonna was influenced by Marilyn.

Marilyn Monroe is featured on this "Legends of Hollywood" postage stamp.

Several Marilyn Monroe fan clubs exist around the United States. Marilyn's image—her platinum-blond hair and glamorous gowns, her lipstick-red lips and bright blue eyes—can be found almost anywhere in the world. The pop artist Andy Warhol painted a famous picture of Marilyn. Singer Elton John wrote a song for her called "Candle in the Wind."

Some stars have copied Marilyn's looks and style. Pop singer Madonna, in particular, was strongly influenced by

Andy Warhol painted Marilyn in 1967.

Marilyn. Madonna borrowed Marilyn's blond hair and sex-symbol image—but added confidence and invulnerability to her style, qualities Marilyn lacked.

In 1995 the U.S. Postal Service paid special tribute to Marilyn Monroe. They honored her with a 32-cent postage stamp that features a glamorous painting of her.

Marilyn was never very comfortable with her celebrity image. She once said, "Please don't make me a joke." She wanted more than anything to be taken seriously.

Marilyn Monroe accomplished something that few people in history have done. She became a cultural icon. Marilyn is bigger than life. She is admired with great devotion. Though she has passed away, her name is as well known as that of any living person.

After Marilyn's death, her friend Susan Strasberg wrote, "Now Marilyn is like one of those stars we look up at to make wishes on. It has died, but its light is still traveling toward us."

Marilyn will continue to shine, now and always, more brilliantly than she ever could have imagined.

S O U R C E S

12 "To Aristophanes and Back," *Time* (May 14, 1956), 74.

14 Marilyn Monroe, *My Story* (New York: Stein and Day, 1974), 18.

14 Ibid., 9.

14 "To Aristophanes and Back," 76.

15 Monroe, *My Story,* 11.

19 *Marilyn and the Camera* (Boston: Little, Brown, 1989), 14.

19 Monroe, *My Story,* 14.

20 To Aristophanes and Back," 76.

21 Ibid.

21 Monroe, *My Story,* 15.

22 Ibid.

22 Marilyn Monroe in the Milton Greene papers, Collection 2, File IX, Folder 22, 4.

25 Monroe, *My Story,* 20.

25 Gloria Steinem and George Barris, *Marilyn: Norma Jeane* (New York: Henry Holt, 1986), 181–182.

28 Randall Riese and Neal Hitchens,*The Unabridged Marilyn* (New York: Congdon & Weed, 1987), 286.

28 Steinem, *Marilyn: Norma Jeane,* 39–40.

32 Monroe, *My Story,* 25.

35 Donald Spoto, *Marilyn Monroe: The Biography* (New York: HarperCollins, 1993), 70.

36 Ibid., 73.

37 Berniece Baker Miracle and Mona Rae Miracle, *My Sister Marilyn: A Memoir of Marilyn Monroe* (Chapel Hill, N.C.: Algonquin Books of Chapel Hill, 1994), 128.

39 Spoto, *Marilyn Monroe: The Biography,* 79.

41 Fred L. Guiles, *Legend: The Life and Death of Marilyn Monroe* (New York: Stein and Day), 78.

51 Monroe, *My Story,* 31.

51 "To Aristophanes and Back," 79.

53 Anthony Summers, *Goddess: The Secret Lives of Marilyn Monroe* (New York: Macmillan, 1985), 13.

55 Guiles, *Legend: The Life and Death of Marilyn Monroe,* 99.

57 Maurice Zolotow, *Billy Wilder in Hollywood* (New York: Putnam, 1977).

57 Summers, *Goddess: The Secret Lives of Marilyn Monroe,* 27.

58 Spoto, *Marilyn Monroe: The Biography,* 114.

63 Guiles, *Legend: The Life and Death of Marilyn Monroe,* 119.

65 Natasha Lytess with Jane Wilkie, *My Years With Marilyn* (Unpublished manuscript, Zolotow Collection, University of Texas, Austin), 4.

67 Summers, *Goddess: The Secret Lives of Marilyn Monroe,* 51.

70 Riese and Hitchens, *The Unabridged Marilyn,* 225.

70 Steinem and Barris, *Marilyn: Norma Jeane,* 123.

71 "To Aristophanes and Back," 80.

72 Riese and Hitchens, *The Unabridged Marilyn,* 372.

74 Clare Booth Luce, "What Really Killed Marilyn," *Life* (August 7, 1964), 72.

79 Monroe, *My Story,* 125.

80 Ibid., 126.

81 Ibid.

82 Summers, *Goddess: The Secret Lives of Marilyn Monroe,* 68.

82–83 Spoto, *Marilyn Monroe: The Biography,* 259.

83 Monroe, *My Story,* 139.

86 Spoto, *Marilyn Monroe: The Biography,* 265.

89 "Life Goes to a Select Supper for Marilyn," *Life* (Nov. 22, 1954), 162.

90 Monroe, *My Story,* 32.

93 "To Aristophanes and Back," 80.

94 Riese and Hitchens, *The Unabridged Marilyn,* 501.

94 Susan Strasberg, *Marilyn and Me: Sisters, Rivals, Friends* (New York: Warner Books, 1992), 29.

94 Ibid., 35.

98 Guiles, *Legend: The Life and Death of Marilyn Monroe,* 470.

101 Lena Pepitone, *Marilyn Monroe Confidential* (New York, Simon & Schuster, 1979), 61.

101 Strasberg, *Marilyn and Me: Sisters, Rivals, Friends,* 118.

101 Ibid., 119.

102 Steinem and Barris, *Marilyn: Norma Jeane,* 199.

109 Robert LaGuardia, *Monty: A Biography of Montgomery Clift* (New York: Avon Books, 1977), 118.

110 "The Legend of Marilyn Monroe," Wolper Productions, 1967.

113 Summers, *Goddess: The Secret Lives of Marilyn Monroe,* 359.

114 "I Love You . . . I Love You," *Newsweek* (August 20, 1962), 30.

FILMOGRAPHY OF MARILYN MONROE

Scudda-Hoo! Scudda-Hay!
Twentieth Century-Fox
Directed by F. Hugh Herbert
Released April 1948

The Fireball
Twentieth Century-Fox
Directed by Tay Garnett
Released November 1950

Dangerous Years
Twentieth Century-Fox
Directed by Arthur Pierson
Released December 1947

Right Cross
Metro-Goldwyn-Mayer
Directed by John Sturges
Released November 1950

Ladies of the Chorus
Columbia Studios
Directed by Phil Karlson
Released October 1948

Home Town Story
Metro-Goldwyn-Mayer
Directed by Arthur Pierson
Released May 1951

Love Happy
United Artists
Directed by David Miller
Released April 1950

As Young As You Feel
Twentieth Century-Fox
Directed by Harmon Jones
Released August 1951

A Ticket to Tomahawk
Twentieth Century-Fox
Directed by Richard Sale
Released May 1950

Love Nest
Twentieth Century-Fox
Directed by Joseph Newman
Released October 1951

The Asphalt Jungle
Metro-Goldwyn-Mayer
Directed by John Huston
Released May 1950

Let's Make It Legal
Twentieth Century-Fox
Directed by Richard Sale
Released November 1951

All About Eve
Twentieth Century-Fox
Directed by
Joseph L. Mankiewicz
Released October 1950

Clash by Night
RKO
Directed by Fritz Lang
Released June 1952

We're Not Married
Twentieth Century-Fox
Directed by Edmund Goulding
Released July 1952

Don't Bother to Knock
Twentieth Century-Fox
Directed by Roy Baker
Released July 1952

Monkey Business
Twentieth Century-Fox
Directed by Howard Hawks
Released September 1952

O. Henry's Full House
Twentieth Century-Fox
Directed by Henry Koster
Released October 1952

Niagara
Twentieth Century-Fox
Directed by Henry Hathaway
Released January 1953

Gentleman Prefer Blondes
Twentieth Century-Fox
Directed by Howard Hawks
Released July 1953

How To Marry a Millionaire
Twentieth Century-Fox
Directed by Jean Negulesco
Released November 1953

River of No Return
Twentieth Century-Fox
Directed by Otto Preminger
Released April 1954

There's No Business Like Show Business
Twentieth Century-Fox
Directed by Walter Lang
Released December 1954

The Seven Year Itch
Twentieth Century-Fox
Directed by Billy Wilder
Released June 1955

Bus Stop
Twentieth Century-Fox
Directed by Joshua Logan
Released August 1956

The Prince and the Showgirl
Produced by Laurence Olivier
and Milton H. Greene for
Warner Brothers
Directed by Laurence Olivier
Released June 1957

Some Like It Hot
United Artists
Directed by Billy Wilder
Released March 1959

Let's Make Love
Twentieth Century-Fox
Directed by George Cukor
Released September 1960

The Misfits
United Artists
Directed by John Huston
Released February 1961

BIBLIOGRAPHY

Cowie, Peter. *Seventy Years of Cinema.* South Brunswick, N.J.: A.S. Barnes & Co., 1969.

Guiles, Fred L. *Legend: The Life and Death of Marilyn Monroe.* New York: Stein and Day, 1984.

LaGuardia, Robert. *Monty: A Biography of Montgomery Clift.* New York: Arbor House, 1977.

Lytess, Natasha, with Jane Wilkie. *My Years with Marilyn.* Unpublished manuscript. Zolotow Collection, University of Texas, Austin.

Mailer, Norman. *Marilyn, the Classic.* New York: Galahad Books, 1988.

Marilyn and the Camera. Foreword by Jane Russell. Boston: Little, Brown, 1989.

Miracle, Berniece Baker, and Mona Rae Miracle. *My Sister Marilyn: A Memoir of Marilyn Monroe.* Chapel Hill, N.C.: Algonquin Books of Chapel Hill, 1994.

Monroe, Marilyn. *My Story.* New York: Stein and Day, 1974.

Pepitone, Lena. *Marilyn Monroe Confidential.* New York: Simon and Schuster, 1979.

Riese, Randall, and Neal Hitchens. *The Unabridged Marilyn.* New York: Congdon & Weed, 1987.

Shaw, Sam, and Norman Rosten. *Marilyn Among Friends.* New York: Henry Holt & Co., 1988.

Spoto, Donald. *Marilyn Monroe: The Biography.* New York: HarperCollins, 1993.

Steinem, Gloria, and George Barris. *Marilyn: Norma Jeane.* New York: Henry Holt & Co., 1986.

Strasberg, Susan. *Marilyn and Me: Sisters, Rivals, Friends.* New York: Warner Books, 1992.

Summers, Anthony. *Goddess: The Secret Lives of Marilyn Monroe.* New York: Macmillan, 1985.

Taylor, Roger. *Marilyn Monroe: In Her Own Words.* New York: Putnam, 1983.

Zolotow, Maurice. *Billy Wilder in Hollywood.* New York: Putnam, 1977.

Magazines and Newspaper Articles

"A Constellation Is Born." *Newsweek,* October 31, 1960, 90.

"I Love You... I Love You." *Newsweek*, August 20, 1962, 30.

"Life Goes to a Select Supper for Marilyn." *Life,* November 22, 1954, 162.

Luce, Clare Booth. "What Really Killed Marilyn." *Life,* August 7, 1964, 68.

Meryman, Richard, and Allan Grant. "Marilyn Monroe: The Last Interview." *Life,* August 1992, 72.

Smith, Liz. "What Becomes a Legend Most?" *McCall's,* July 1992, 115.

Spoto, Donald. "Marilyn Monroe: The Nomadic Life of a Screen Legend." *Architectural Digest,* April 1994, 230.

"To Aristophanes and Back." *Time,* May 14, 1956, 74.

"Who's a Misfit?" *Newsweek,* September 12, 1960, 102.

Marilyn Monroe starred with Don Murray in Bus Stop *(1956).*

PHOTO ACKNOWLEDGMENTS

Photographs are used with permission of: Archive Photos, pp. 2, 9, 13, 16, 64, 76, 85, 91, 95, 99, 103, 106, 111; SuperStock, pp. 6, 40, 45, 52, 112; UPI/Corbis-Bettmann, p. 10 (top); UPI/Bettmann, pp. 10 (bottom), 38, 56, 59, 78, 81, 83, 84, 88, 92, 104; The Bettmann Archive, pp. 18, 61, 66, 97; Independent Picture Service, p. 23; Archive Photos/Hurrell/Creative Art Images, p. 24; Seth Poppel Yearbook Archives, p. 26; Wisconsin Center for Film and Theater Research, p. 31; Archive Photos/Frank Driggs, pp. 33, 68, 69; Springer/Bettmann Film Archive, pp. 34, 50; © 733548 Ontario Limited, p. 44; YWCA of the U.S.A./National Board Archives, p. 49; Archive Photos/Popperfotos, p. 54; Hollywood Book and Poster, pp. 60, 75, 77, 87, 100, 102, 108, 128; Springer/Corbis-Bettmann, p. 73; Archive Photos/Darlene Hammond, p. 90; Reuters/Corbis-Bettmann, p. 114; U.S. Postal Service, p. 115; Tate Gallery, London/Art Resource, NY, p. 116.

Front cover photograph used with permission of UPI/Bettmann. Back cover photograph used with permission of Archive Photos.

ABOUT THE AUTHOR

Katherine Krohn, a graduate of the University of Michigan, writes biographies for young readers, news articles, and fiction. She has also written and produced an award-winning cable television series. She lives in Eugene, Oregon.

Lerner's **Newsmakers** series:

Muhammad Ali: Champion

Ray Charles: Soul Man

The 14th Dalai Lama: Spiritual Leader of Tibet

Sir Edmund Hillary: To Everest and Beyond

Marilyn Monroe: Norma Jeane's Dream

Steven Spielberg: Master Storyteller